Every Day Is A New Day

A Journey To Finding Your Inner Light

Kacee Allard

kaceejo.com

ISBN: 1536832332
ISBN-13: 9781536832334

DEDICATION

This book is dedicated to my family, who inspires me each and every day to become a more loving, generous, and caring person. Their endless love and laughter allows me to live a life so full of joy and happiness. How I became so lucky is a mystery to me.

My mom, Stacey, is the person who motivated me to accomplish this journal. Her encouragement and assistance is like no one else's. I can only dream of becoming as strong, determined, and loving as she is. She is beautiful in every way and I am beyond blessed to call her mom. I will love her forever and ever.

My dad, Ron, has made me into the person I am today. The amount of love in his heart is beyond explanation. He is the person who makes me laugh when I could cry. He is the person who picks me up when I have never been so down. My dad is my hero and to say I am blessed to have him would be an understatement. I somehow became the luckiest girl in the world to have a dad like him. I will love him forever and ever.

My younger sister, Kelli, keeps my feet on the ground when my head is in the sky. She is such a beautiful person inside and out. Her heart is so big and her generosity is astounding. To watch her grow into the young woman she is today has been the biggest pleasure and gift. She is my go to. She is my best friend. She is everything now that she will ever need to be. And I will love her forever and ever.

I'm grateful for every friend who has ever walked in or walked out of my life. My friends, from age ranges 17-80, have taught me that we are all in the same boat. Age is just a number and we all want the same thing—to be happy. I want to give a special thanks to my friends Lauren, Grace, Leigh, Kay, Kelsey, and Alicia for allowing me to be my true, authentic self. The person I must express the most gratefulness for is Marilyn. Marilyn has allowed to shine my inner light for all to see. Her own light has inspired me to not only write this journal, but follow my dreams and never doubt my instincts.

To the people I love with all my heart: my grandparents, aunts, uncles, and cousins. The amount of love and laughter that has been shared over my eighteen years is more than most people experience in a lifetime. They have taught me to cherish every breath, laugh, and, tear. They are my everything, because family is forever.

The last people I must express my gratitude for are my two deceased uncles, Al and Don. Ever since they have departed, I have never doubted their strong presence I feel each and every day. They are my angels. I will remember and cherish every laugh and joke ever exchanged. The world has changed without them on it, but it has also changed just by knowing they are watching over it. This journal was titled from the wise words of my Uncle Donnie. I hope you all enjoy it to the fullest and feel the incredible sensation of internal content.

1. Think of someone you owe great thanks to and write down exactly what you are thankful for. Then, take a card and write that person a thank you and send it.

_____

_____

_____

_____

_____

_____

_____

_____

_____

_____

_____

_____

_____

_____

_____

2. Write out one, or all, of your regrets in life. Then, rip out this page, tear it apart, and completely forget these regrets ever existed. They are a part of the past and there is no changing it.

_____

_____

_____

_____

_____

_____

_____

_____

_____

_____

_____

_____

_____

_____

_____

Kacee Allard

3.   Name a song that you swear was written personally for
     you and why you believe so.

4. Who makes the greater impact on society: the writer or the reader? Why?

5.   If two people were to have a conversation about you, what would they say? What do you wish they would say? Take the actions necessary so it is not a matter of whether people would say what you wish, but rather knowing they will.

6. You are suddenly granted one million dollars and must use it to travel the world. What is your route?

7. Who is the person who knows you better than you know yourself, or at least close to that? Explain your relationship with that person.

8.   Write out a list of what you are an expert on. What do these things mean to you? Are they your passions? Hobbies? Values?

9. What is the earliest memory you have of your life? What is the importance of this memory to you?

_____

_____

_____

_____

_____

_____

_____

_____

_____

_____

_____

_____

_____

_____

_____

10.   If everything in the world could only be one color, what color would it be? What things would be most beautiful in that color?

11.   Write about a movie that made you cry like a baby. If you've never cried at a movie, watch *Me Before You.* That shit will make you cry.

12. Give a stranger a genuine compliment. Write about how you think it made that person feel and why everyone deserves a good compliment.

13. How big do you think this world really is? Write about how a person could possibly know this. On a clear night, lie beneath the stars and you will get a small glimpse.

_____

_____

_____

_____

_____

_____

_____

_____

_____

_____

_____

_____

_____

_____

_____

14.　Write about a moment in your life that you will never
　　　forget.

Kacee Allard

15. Recall a time when someone said or did something vicious to you. Write it down, and, once again, rip it out and tear it apart. The past is the past. Forgive and forget.

_____

_____

_____

_____

_____

_____

_____

_____

_____

_____

_____

_____

_____

16. Create your own original life motto. Why should everyone live by your motto?

17.   Who is the most important person in your life? Why?

18.   Would you consider yourself an introvert or extrovert? Explain your reasoning. Regardless of your conclusion, learn to love what you are, there is no right or wrong.

19.	What is the outfit you feel the best in? If you don't have a favorite outfit, get one. You deserve to feel good!

20.   What is the wildest dream you have ever had?

21.   Write about the most important lesson you have learned
      about life.

22.   Write what this word means to you: STRENGTH

23. You have to give someone the ultimate care package. What is in it?

24.   It has been said that a picture is worth a thousand words. Insert a picture in this journal and write a list of thirty words (because one-thousand is a lot) that describe anything associated with the picture.

25.   Today is your last day to live. What do you do? Who do
       you see? What is your last meal? What is the last song
       you listen to? Who do you say "I love you" to?

Kacee Allard

26. Write all of the qualities, both physical and internal, that
     you believe would make the ideal human.

27. Recall and write about a time you could have sworn you were in a dream.

28.   Briefly write your life story. When the time feels right,
       share yours with another person and ask about theirs.

29. Write about a time you put your whole heart and soul into something.

30. Starting tomorrow you have to start teaching a class of
students until the day you die. The class can be based
off of any topic in the world. What issue, subject, theory,
idea, etc. do you teach about? Why?

31.   Write an open-hearted letter to someone you have lost or
       someone you miss dearly.

32. Find a random ticket from absolutely any event and write
     about any memories you have about that event. Stick the
     ticket in your journal.

33.   Create a bucket list.

_____

_____

_____

_____

_____

_____

_____

_____

_____

_____

_____

_____

_____

_____

_____

34. Write out a list of songs that would be on a playlist titled "Rainy Day."

35. Write out a list of songs that would be on a playlist titled "Because I'm Happy."

36. If you could eliminate one feeling/emotion from the world
     what would it be?

37. Close your eyes and block out all that is around you for thirty seconds. What are the first thoughts that come to your mind? Are they people, places, memories? Write them down.

38. How do you like to spend your free time? What do think
    this says about you?

39.   Write out a list of ten amazing things about yourself.

40. If you were afraid of absolutely nothing, what things would you do?

41. Make a list of rules to live by. I will share mine with you.

1. Love yourself unconditionally.
2. Accept your flaws—every person has them.
3. Don't chase your dream, live your dream.
4. Live and let live.
5. Be somebody who makes everybody feel like a somebody.
6. Know that a light heart lives long.
7. Always appreciate the beauty of nature and never mistreat it.
8. Enjoy the sunshine.
9. Don't take yourself too seriously, no one else ever will.
10. When you are having a bad day, open a book and read to escape reality for just a while.
11. Understand that everything happens for a reason. There is no such thing as coincidence.

42. What is something someone told you never to do, but you did it anyway? Why did you do it?

43. What was something that you swore was killing you but
was actually making you stronger?

44. Write about a time you felt inspired by another person and acted on that inspiration.

45.   Name some beliefs you will always stand firm by.

46. If you were to write a novel, what would it be about? Give a
     brief story line.

47. Write about a book you believe everyone should read and why. Here is mine: Don't Sweat the Small Stuff... And It's All Small Stuff.

48. If you were allowed to live in only one place for the rest of your life, where would it be? Why there?

49. Write about an opportunity you took that made a big
difference in your life.

50. What is one thing you struggle with daily? Write a strategy
to fixing that struggle. Now put the strategy to work!

51. Write about a time that someone wished you luck and it really carried through. Now, take a penny and place it on the ground heads up so someone else can have good luck.

52. If you could put an end to anything—a controversy, an idea, a problem—what would it be? Why do you want to end it?

53. Why do you think people have always felt the urge to judge the actions, looks, and words of others? Do you believe there is logic and reasoning behind the judgements?

54.   What is it that makes each person his or her own? Is it
     looks, personality, beliefs, culture?

55. On this page, write a letter to your very best friend.
     Express whatever comes from your heart. Whether or
     not you decide to share this with the friend is your
     decision!

56. What is the one thing you hope to accomplish before you
     die?

57. Write about various times you were rejected in life and how you have grown and learned from them.

58. Write about a miracle you have witnessed.

59.   Write about a time you found something you lost and
      never expected to find.

Kacee Allard

60. Write about something society has placed too much value on.

61.   Think about a time when someone you know was placed in
       a very difficult situation and how he or she handled it.
       How can you learn from his or her actions?

Kacee Allard

62. Write about a tradition you have with family or a friend and the importance of the tradition to you.

63. You are granted $1,000,000 and you must use it in a
    philanthropic way. Who do you give to?

64. What is something that has yet to be invented, but would
     change the world?

65. Write a pep talk that could get anyone feeling better on a
     bad day.

66. What is something you have accomplished that you will be proud of forever?

67. Is there someone who has left a lasting impression on you? How so?

68. If you were to compare today's generation to an older generation, what things would you compare? Name similarities and differences. In your opinion, is there a better generation?

69. Write about a "title" you have been given that is important to you? Explain.

_____

_____

_____

_____

_____

_____

_____

_____

_____

_____

_____

_____

_____

_____

_____

70. If you are a smart phone user, download the Daily Horoscope app. Make a habit of looking at your horoscope, and one day when it is freakishly accurate, write about it.

71. Write about something you would like to transform into a habit. Write how you can incorporate it into your daily schedule and get to work!

72. What is something you enjoy doing that probably no one
    else enjoys doing?

73. When you want to enjoy some quality time with yourself, what do you do? Do you see the value in this time? You must value it.

74.   I was once told to stop "should-ing" myself. So I did. I no
      longer say I "should" do something—I just do it. What
      are some things you need to stop "should-ing" yourself
      about?

75. Would you rather live a life without imagination or a life without inspiration?

76. Write about how an ideal summer would be spent.

77.　Create a list of wise words and sayings assuring you that everything will turn out fine.

78. Which do you value the most: quality time, reassuring words, kind gestures, or thoughtful gifts?

79.   Which is more important—a good book or a good music
      album? Why?

80. What is the best thing you have ever created with your own hands?

Kacee Allard

81.   What do you think is the most valuable thing in life? It can
      be a person, feeling, idea, object, anything.

82. List thirteen reasons why you are living a great life.

83.   What is the perfect way to spend a Sunday morning?

84. Describe what you think the word "spirituality" means. Now relate it to you and your own spirit.

85. How do you express your creativity? Do you write, draw, paint, dance, sing, sculpt? Write about how it makes you feel.

86. Write about a time you were very generous to someone.

87.   What are some things that are free but should be paid for?

88. Write about the climax of your life so far.

_____

_____

_____

_____

_____

_____

_____

_____

_____

_____

_____

_____

_____

_____

89. Write about an experience you have had that you think everyone else needs to have.

90.   Is it better to be full of answers or full of curiosity?

91. What is the best year ever to have passed? Whether you
     learned of it or lived it, explain your reasoning.

92. Write about the place that makes you feel most at home.
    Who is there with you? How do you feel when you're
    there?

93. Is there a story behind your name? What is it you love about your name? How does it fit you?

94.   What is your spirit animal? Why?

95.   Write about a way that you can enhance your knowledge
      of the world around you. Why is it helpful to know and
      understand other cultures and ways of living?

96. Write about a time you put another person before yourself.

97. What is something you think everyone should take the time to do each day? Explain.

98. What is the most beautiful thing you have ever seen? Write
about the experience.

99. What was the most adventurous thing you have ever done?

100. Do you feel you understand yourself better after writing in this journal? What new things have you learned about yourself?

Kacee Allard

Every Day Is A New Day

219

Every Day Is A New Day

233

Every Day Is A New Day

243

Kacee Allard

Kacee Allard

Kacee Allard

Parting Words

From the bottom of my heart, I would like to thank each individual who purchased this journal. Every prompt was written with the intention to not only better yourself, but to simply know yourself. I hope life is nothing but wonderful to all of you and that we can cross paths during our life journeys. Love yourself and love all those around you. Life is too short to feel anything but love. Now go live a life worth living.

Made in the USA
Middletown, DE
20 February 2017